Drunkard's Path

Stepping Beyond

Cheryl Phillips & Karla Schulz

Dedicated to
Cinda Farrell
Thanks for the joy and
wonder you left behind.

Graphic Design by Brooke Jeschke

Quilts by
Karla Schulz: 44, 46, 47 , 48 b, 49 c, 51 a b, 53, 54 a b, 55 b, 56, 57 a b, 59
Cheryl Phillips: 45, 49 b, 52 a b c,
Cinda Farrell: 48 a
Denise Lassiter-Vachon: 49 a, 58
Kathy Moorhead-Johnson: 50 a b
Sandra Brown: 55 a c
Vivian Head machine quilted: 45, 52 a b c, 53, 54 b

Fabrics:
Lakehouse Fabrics
Northcott Fabrics

Printed by Colorado Printing, Grand Junction, Colorado

Contents

Walk the Cut A Round Path to curved success.

The traditional Drunkard's Path forms the
foundation for our journey.
Step beyond tradition to explore new creative paths.

Our destination is inspiration!

The stepping stones to our new framed path:
Sew a circle into a square;
Cut it into fourths;
and you have four Drunkard's Path Blocks at once.

It's easier and more accurate than piecing one block at a time,
(although you still have the option of making Single Blocks).

Continue along the path and make
Path in the Corner Blocks,
Half Rectangles,
or Ringed Blocks.

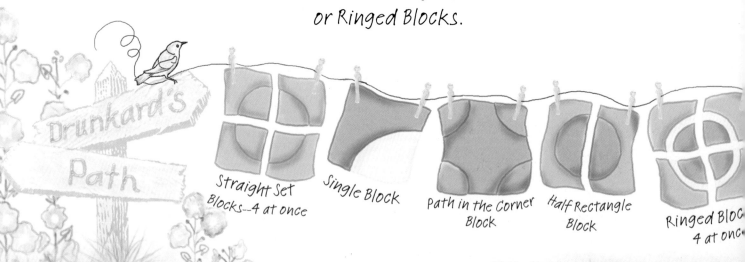

Drunkard's Path

Straight Set
Blocks--4 at once

Single Block

Path in the Corner
Block

Half Rectangle
Block

Ringed Block
4 at once

4

Follow a different route:
Sew a circle into a square, but this time cut it diagonally into fourths and you'll have four Drunkard's Path Triangles.

Sew the four Drunkard's Path Triangles together to make two pieced Double Path Blocks.

Or make the Double Path Block individually.

Double Path Blocks can be combined with Uneven Double Path and Half Diagonal Blocks.

Single block options are ideal for speciality fabrics such as stripes, novelty prints or large florals.

The possibilities are endless!

Circle Sally is your tour guide.

Triangle Blocks
4 at once

Double Path
Block

Uneven Double
Path Block

Half Diagonal
Blocks
2 at once

Flat Circles

The traditional way to sew a Drunkard's Path is one block at a time. Our new framed circle path creates four blocks at once. First you sew a circle into a frame. Next you cut it into fourths, then sew it back together again.

If the set in circle is a *true* circle, it won't remain true when you've sewn it back together because of the seam allowances. To solve the dilemma, let's look at how a traditional block is drafted.

To properly draft a Drunkard's Path block, you draw the block, cut it apart and add ¼" seams allowance to all sides.

For the framed circle method you'll want to begin with the seam allowances added to the center of the circle. It gives your circle a *"flat spot"* on the center top, center bottom, and both sides. This is easily accomplished with the amazing *Cut A Round* tool. When the flat circle is framed, cut into fourths and resewn, the new block has a circle that is perfectly round.

A Drunkard's Path Block

Block pieces with seam allowance added

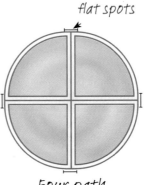

Four path units placed together

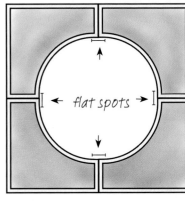

Four frame units placed together

See how you have a true circle when resewn together?

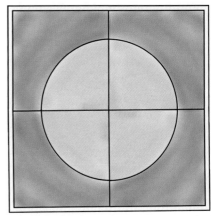

4 patch block sewn together

A framed true circle

A framed circle cut into fourths

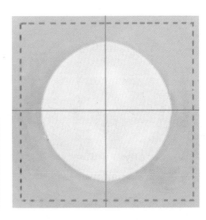

Resewn together

See how you do NOT have a true circle when sewn together?

6

Tools
The *Cut A Round*

The *Cut A Round* tool made by Phillips Fiber Art is ideal for circular cutting. The portable midi *Cut A Round* tool cuts circles 4" to 12". The standard *Cut A Round* tool cuts circles 6" to 19" in diameter.

The *Cut A Round* tool is a versatile tool for cutting any of the Drunkard's Path variations shown in the book. One tool for all the sizes, so it eliminates individual templates. The *Cut A Round* cutting slots keep your rotary cutter in the correct placement, whereas your cutter easily drifts away from the edge of a standard template. It is important to hold your rotary cutter vertical as you cut along the slot. When cutting standard strips, you tend to push the cutter through the fabric. With the *Cut A Round* you need to slow it down a bit and cut with downward pressure. Accurate cutting is crucial for your success.

The tool can be used for cutting perfect circles, but please note in this book we won't be using the fold line, rather we'll use the ¼" seam allowance line for all of our cutting, unless otherwise noted.

To find the tool, contact your local quilt shop or go to www.phillipsfiberart.com. Product information is listed on page 64.

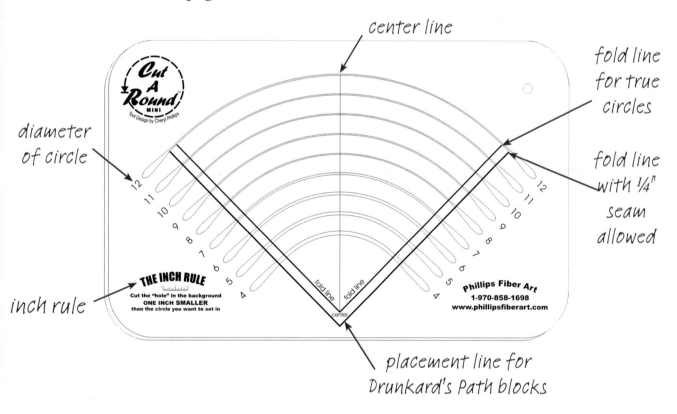

center line

fold line for true circles

fold line with ¼" seam allowed

diameter of circle

inch rule

placement line for Drunkard's Path blocks

Templates

You can substitute the templates found on pages 60-63 for the *Cut A Round* tool. Trace the templates onto freezer paper. Iron the paper onto your fabric, then cut out both paper and fabric in one step. Scissors will work better than a rotary cutter here. Keep in mind how important it is to be accurate with your cutting.

Fabric and Thread

Quality 100% cotton fabrics and threads are suggested for your Drunkards Path project.

When choosing fabrics, remember sharply contrasting values provide the most dramatic paths, while fabrics without a strong value difference offer an opportunity to blend colors and values for a romantic look.

Block sizes were chosen to be fat quarter friendly. Allow extra fabric for directional fabrics and fussy cutting repetitive designs. These fabrics may dictate cutting the Drunkard's Path Blocks individually.

If you preshrink your fabric, iron it thoroughly **before** cutting your block components. If you do not preshrink, misting the fabric and pressing with a hot iron should compensate for shrinkage. Spray starch or sizing gives the fabrics extra stability and is helpful with curved piecing.

Grain line

Grain line is of particular importance when making Drunkard's Path Blocks. The crosswise grain is rotated to match the lengthwise grain in Drunkard's Path Blocks. Rotating grain is suggested to allow the fabric to "ease" as you sew the circle into the frame, creating less chance of bumps or puckers in the circular seam.

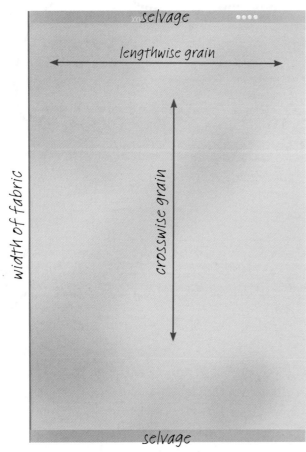

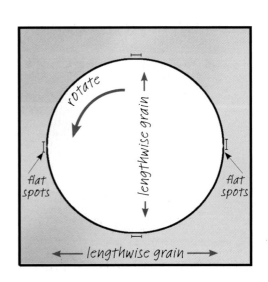

Rulers

A 6" x 24" ruler is best for cutting blocks into fourths. It's helpful to have a ruler with 45 degree markings.

A 12 ½" square ruler is helpful for cutting background squares. An 8 ½" square is useful for some block sizes.

Rotary Cutter

A 45 mm rotary cutter is recommended for both the standard and the portable midi *Cut A Round* tools. You may find the smaller 28 mm cutter useful when using the midi tool for circles under 7". Circular cutting is much easier if the blade is sharp, so it's a great time for a new rotary cutting blade.

Cutting Mat

Is your cutting mat smooth, clean and free of groves? If not, you'll have a difficult time cutting smoothly. A good mat is as important as a new rotary cutting blade.

Pins

Is your pin dish a collection of bent, dull pins, and maybe a paper clip or two? Pick through your pin collection and find eight of your sharpest, finest and longest pins. To set in a circle you need just eight pins. This might be a great time to treat yourself to some new ones and throw out the oldies.

Presser Feet

Quarter Inch presser foot

Does your machine have a special ¼" foot? You'll need one because exact ¼" seams are crucial to setting in circles that will lie flat. The math behind the "inch rule" depends on the accuracy of the ¼" seam. If your seams are not accurate, the circle and frame will pucker, distort and not lie flat.

Curve Master presser foot

The Curve Master foot is specially designed for piecing curves. See resources page 61. For setting in circle, you will still need to use pins, as it aids in piecing whole circles. The Curved Master Foot is available from www.justcurves.biz.

¼" test
*Cut three strips, each 2" x 5". Sew them together, press the seams and measure. The set measures 5" wide if you've sewn **exact** ¼" wide seams.*

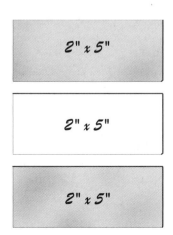

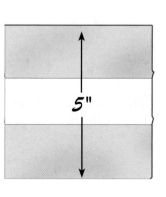

Yardage

The yardages listed in the chart below have been calculated for two color or scrap quilts made with full circle techniques. Quilts made with individual blocks use some what smaller amounts of fabric. Quantities were calculated with only a small amount allowed for straightening. No extra has been allowed for errors. The charts can also be used as a general guideline for your own yardage calculations.

You can combine various block patterns, settings and fabrics choices. Use graph paper to plan your own unique design. To calculate the yardage needed, first count the number of blocks needed, then follow the formula listed below each chart.

Straight Set Blocks

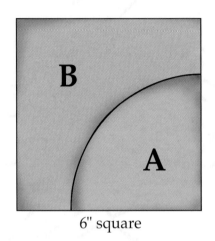

6" square

	Lap/Baby	Twin	Double	Queen
	44" x 55" 80 blocks 8 x 10	66" x 88" 192 blocks 12 x 16	77" x 99" 252 blocks 14 x 18	99" x 110" 360 blocks 18 x 20
Two color version Fabric A	1 ½ yd	3 ½ yd	4 ¾ yd	6 ½ yd
Two color version Fabric B	2 ½ yd	5 ¾ yd	7 ½ yd	10 ¾ yd
OR				
Multiple Colors Scrappy Look	at least 12 fat quarters	at least 36 fat quarters	at least 50 fat quarters	at least 68 fat quarters

The straight set block pictured above is 6" square, finishing at 5 ½". The formula for straight set blocks allows one square of both frame and circle fabric for every **four** blocks. Across the width of 40" wide fabric, you can cut **four** 10" circle squares or **three** 12 ½" frame squares.

To calculate the yardage needed for each fabric chosen for your straight set blocks, follow the formula below:

Quarter circle A

Number of blocks $\div$ **4** = Number of circles*

Number of circles $\div$ **4** = number of 10" wide strips*

Number of 10" wide strips **x 10"** = **yardage needed**

Frame B

Number of blocks $\div$ **4** = Number of frame squares*

Number of frame squares $\div$ **3** = number of 12 ½" wide strips*

Number of 12 ½" strips **x 12.5"** = **yardage needed**

* round up to the nearest whole number

Ringed Blocks

If you're planning on adding a ring to your block, you'll need to buy the same amount for the ring fabric as listed for the A fabric. While the center fabric will take less, be safe and buy the same amount for it.

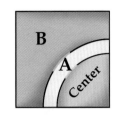

Circle Sally Says:
Going to the quilt shop?
Go ahead--Buy a little extra,
at least 1/4 yd
.....just in case.

Diagonal Set Blocks

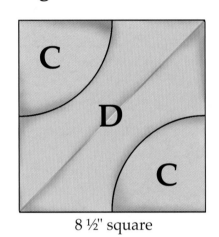

8 ½" square

	Lap/Baby	Twin	Double	Queen
	40" x 48" 30 blocks 5 x 6	72" x 96" 108 blocks 9 x 12	80" x 104" 130 blocks 10 x 13	104" x 112" 182 blocks 13 x 14
Two Color Version Fabric C	1 ¼ yd	4 ⅛ yd	5 yd	6 ¾ yd
Two Color Version Fabric D	1 ⅞ yd	6 ½ yd	8 yd	10 ¾ yd
OR				
Multiple Colors Scrappy Look	at least 14 fat quarters	at least 44 fat quarters	at least 52 fat quarters	at least 72 fat quarters

The diagonal set block pictured above is an 8 ½" square, finishing at 8". The formula for diagonal set blocks allows one square of both frame and circle fabric for every **two** blocks. Across the width of 40" wide fabric, you can cut **four** 10" circle squares or **three** 12 ½" frame squares.

To calculate the yardage needed for each fabric chosen for your diagonal set blocks, follow the formula below:

Quarter circles C

Number of blocks ÷ **2** = Number of circles*

Number of circles ÷ **4** = number of 10" wide strips*

Number of 10" wide strips **x 10" = yardage needed**

Frame D

Number of blocks ÷ **2** = Number of frame squares*

Number of frame squares ÷ **3** = number of 12 ½" wide strips*

Number of 12 ½" strips **x 12.5" = yardage needed**

* round up to the nearest whole number

Straight Set Drunkard's Path
Cutting a Circle

You'll cut a 9" circle from a 10" square of circle fabric.

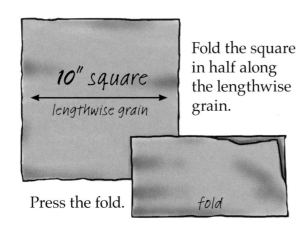

Fold the square in half along the lengthwise grain.

Press the fold.

To make grain lines easy to identify, always make your first fold along the lengthwise grain, to give it the strongest crease.

Fold it in half and press again.

This second fold is along the crosswise grain.

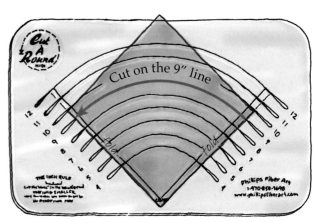

Cut on the 9" line

Place the *Cut A Round* tool on the fabric so the folds are aligned with the ¼" seam allowance lines.

Cut along the 9" curved slot.

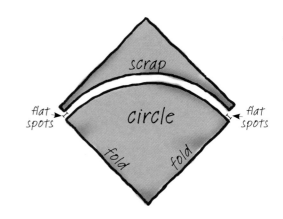

scrap

circle

flat spots

flat spots

fold

fold

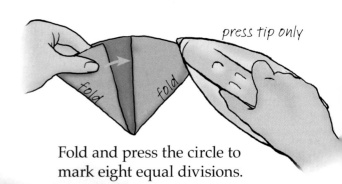

press tip only

fold

fold

Fold and press the circle to mark eight equal divisions.

Straight Set

Circle Sally says:
The key to a perfect circle is folding and pressing the fabric into exact fourths.

Straight Set Drunkard's Path
Cutting a Frame

You'll cut a 8" hole in the 12 ½" square of frame fabric.

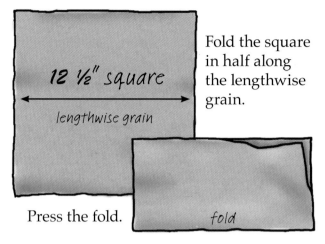

Fold the square in half along the lengthwise grain.

Press the fold.

To make grain lines easy to identify, always make your first fold along the lengthwise grain, to give it the strongest crease.

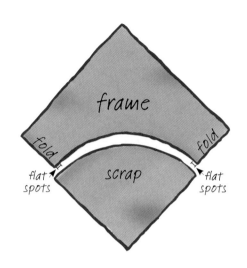

frame

scrap

flat spots   flat spots

fold   fold

Fold it in half and press again.

The second fold is along the crosswise grain.

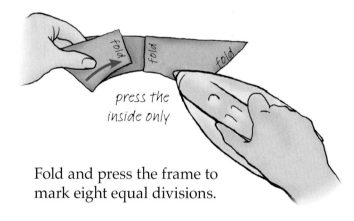

press the inside only

Fold and press the frame to mark eight equal divisions.

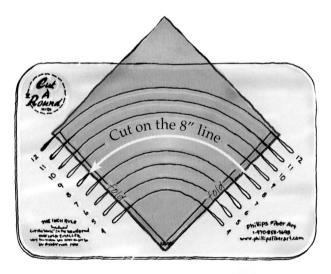

Cut on the 8" line

Place the *Cut A Round* tool on the fabric so the folds are aligned with the ¼" seam allowance lines.

Cut along the 8" curved slot.

Circle Sally says:
The eight folds are match points for your eight pins.

Straight Set

13

Straight Set Drunkard's Path
Framing a Circle

You'll sew the circle into the frame.

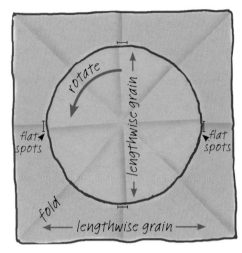

With the circle and frame on a flat surface, rotate the lengthwise grain of the circle perpendicular to the lengthwise grain of the frame.

Bring the frame fabric toward the center of the circle.

Put right sides together and match the fold marks.

Pin each matching fold mark.

just 8 pins!

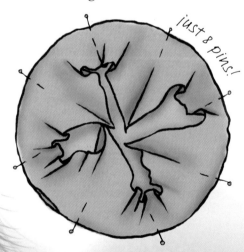

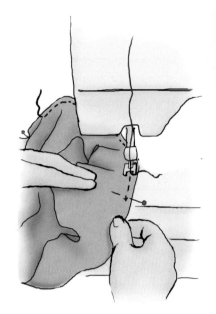

Adjust the edges of the frame to meet the circle. Bumps and uneven seam width will keep your circle from lying flat.

Sew the layers together with an exact ¼" seam. The circle is on the bottom against the bed of the machine and the frame is on top.

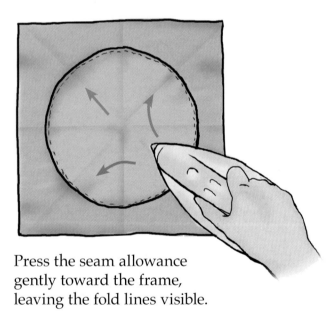

Press the seam allowance gently toward the frame, leaving the fold lines visible.

Circle Sally reminders:

√ ¼" seams must be exact.
√ Use your machine's needle-down feature.
√ The circle goes on bottom.

straight set

14

© Cheryl Phillips and Karla Schulz

Straight Set Drunkard's Path
Cutting Blocks

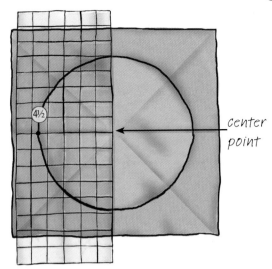

center point

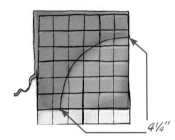

You'll slice the framed circle into fourths.

4¼"

The seam aligns to the 4 ½" lines Trim each block to make an exact 6" square. Trim **only** from the frame sides.

Place the ruler lines parallel to the edges of the fabric with the seam on the 4 ½" line.

Your fold lines will help you align your ruler. Be sure to keep your center point visible.

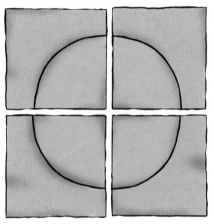

You've completed four traditional Path Blocks at once!

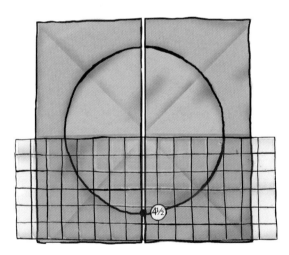

4½

Place the ruler lines parallel to the edges of the fabric with the seam on the 4 ½" line.

Your fold lines will help you align your ruler. Be sure to keep your center point visible.

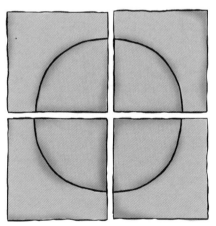

The frame and circle fabrics are reversed for more design possibilities.

Straight Set

Ringed Drunkard's Path

You'll frame a circle in ring fabric.

Fold and press an 8 ½" square of circle fabric into quarters.

8 ½" Square

fold

fold

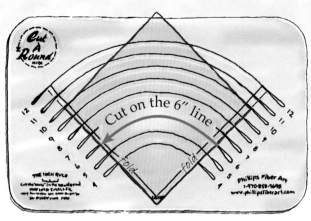

Cut a 6" hole in the ring fabric.

Cut on the 6" line

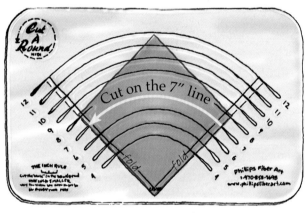

Cut on the 7" line

Cut a 7" circle.

Fold a 10" square of ring fabric into quarters and press.

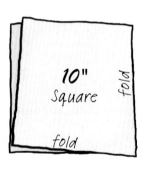

10" Square

fold

fold

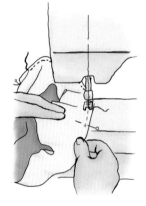

Adjust the edges of the frame to meet the circle. Bumps and uneven seam width will keep your circle from lying flat.

Sew the layers together with exact ¼" seams. The circle goes against the bed of the machine and the frame goes on top.

Press the seam allowance gently toward the frame, leaving the fold lines visible.

Circle Sally Says:
Be sure you frame a circle before trying a ringed one.

Ringed

16

Ringed Drunkard's Path

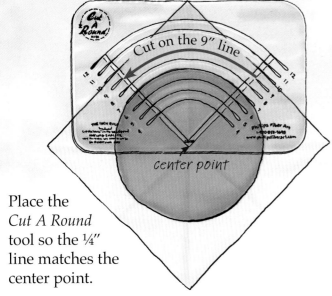

Cut on the 9" line

center point

Place the *Cut A Round* tool so the ¼" line matches the center point.

Cut along the 9" curved slot one layer at a time rather than folding first. This assures the ring is the same size all the way around the circle.

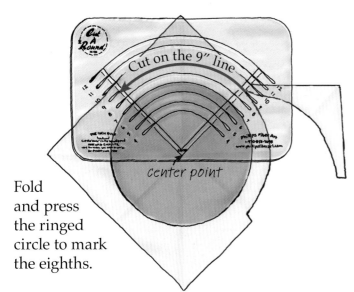

Cut on the 9" line

center point

Fold and press the ringed circle to mark the eighths.

Fold a 12 ½" square of frame fabric into quarters and press.

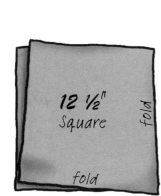

12 ½"
Square

fold

fold

Cut on the 8" line

Cut an 8" hole in the frame square.

Sew the ringed circle into the frame.

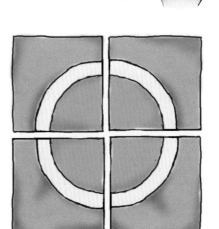

Cut the framed ringed circle into four Drunkard Path Blocks.

Trim each block to 6" Drunkard's Path squares as shown on page 15.

Ringed

Cut single quarter circle and frame.

Single Drunkard's Path Blocks

Quarter Circle
Cut a 5″ square for the quarter circle.

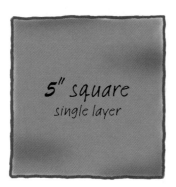

Quarter Frame
Cut a 6″ square for the frame.

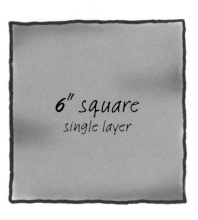

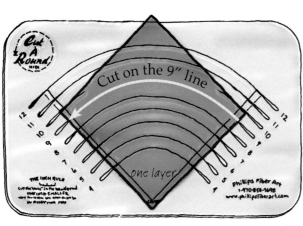

Place the *Cut A Round* tool on top of the fabric square. Align the fabric edge to the ¼″ placement line.
Cut along the 9″ curved slot.

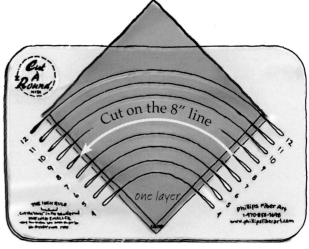

Place the *Cut A Round* tool on top of the fabric square. Align the fabric edge to the ¼″ placement line.
Cut along the 8″ curved slot.

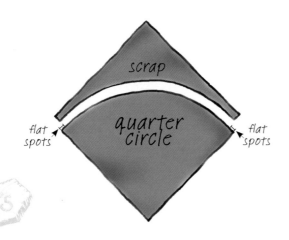

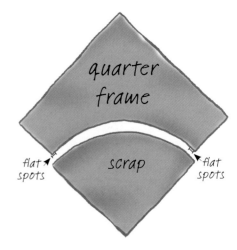

Single

Drunkard's Path

18

Single Drunkard's Path Blocks

You'll make one block at a time.

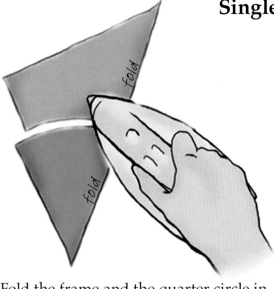

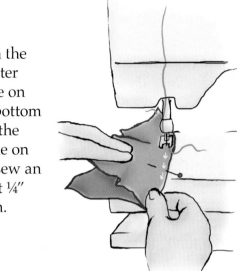

With the quarter circle on the bottom and the frame on top sew an exact ¼″ seam.

Fold the frame and the quarter circle in half along the curved edge to find the center.

Press to mark the center of each piece.

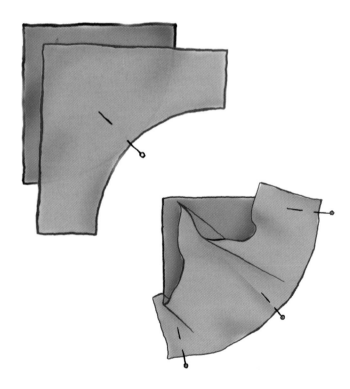

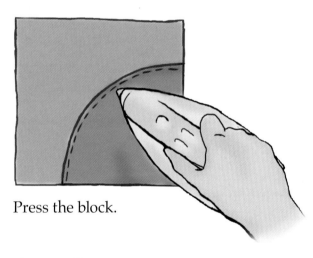

Press the block.

With right sides together match the center marks and pin. Match each side and pin.

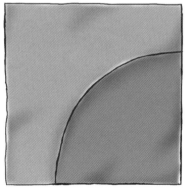

Single Drunkard's Path Block

Single

Path in the Corner

You'll cut away the corners from a square and set in quarters circles.

Cut four 5″ squares for the four quarter circles.

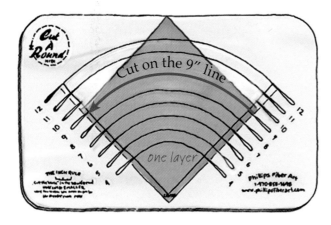

5″ square
four single layers

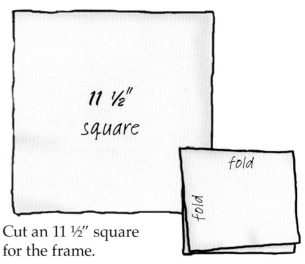

11 ½″ square

fold
fold

Cut an 11 ½″ square for the frame.

Fold the square into quarters.

Place the *Cut A Round* tool on top of the fabric square. Align the fabric edge to the ¼″ placement line.

Cut along the 9″ curved slot.

Cut on the 9″ line
one layer

Place the *Cut A Round* tool on top of the fabric square. Place the folded sides to the top and align the fabric edges to the ¼″ placement line.

Cut along the 8″ curved slot.

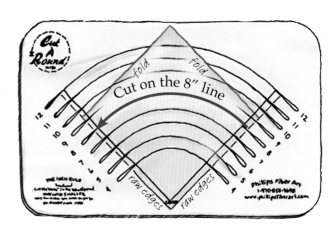

Cut on the 8″ line
fold *fold*
raw edges *raw edges*

Cut **four** quarter circle pieces.

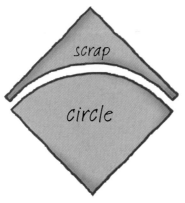

scrap

circle

Cut **one** frame piece.

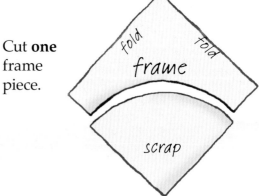

fold *fold*
frame

scrap

Circle Sally says:
Great for large florals, machine embroidery, and photo transfers.

Path in the Corner

You'll make a square with quarter circles in all four corners.

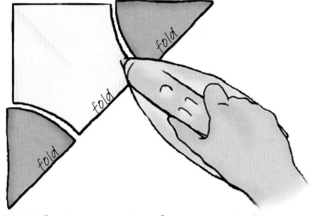

Fold the frame and each quarter circle in half along the curved edge to find the center.

Press to mark the center of each piece.

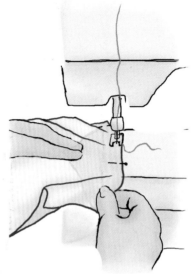

With the quarter circle on the bottom and the frame on top sew an exact ¼″ seam.

Press the block.

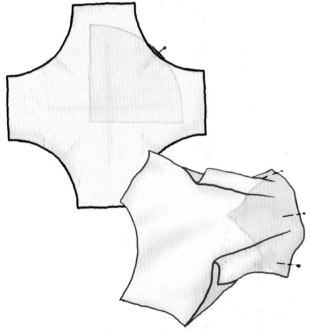

With right sides together match the center marks and pin. Match each side and pin.

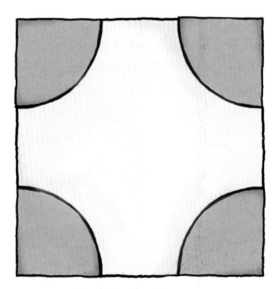

Path in the Corner
Drunkard's Path Block

Path in the Corner

Half Circle Rectangles

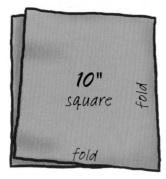

You'll cut a circle and frame both with only two flat spots.

Fold a 10″ square in half along the crosswise grain and press.

Fold the square in half again and press.

Fold a 12 ½″ square in half along the lengthwise grain and press.

Fold the square in half again and press.

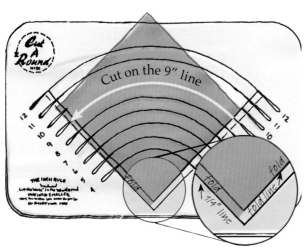

Cut on the 9″ line

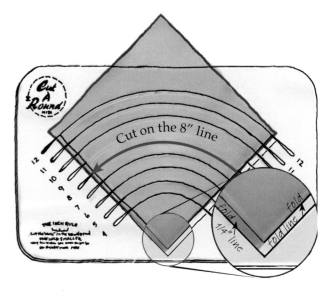

Cut on the 8″ line

Place the *Cut A Round* tool on the fabric so one fold is aligned with the ¼″ seam allowance line and the other fold is aligned with the fold line on the *Cut A Round* tool.

Cut along the 9″ curved slot.

Place the *Cut A Round* tool on the fabric so one fold is aligned with the ¼″ seam allowance line and the other fold is aligned with the fold line on the *Cut A Round* tool.

Cut along the 8″ curved slot.

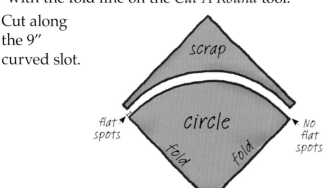

scrap / circle / flat spots / NO flat spots

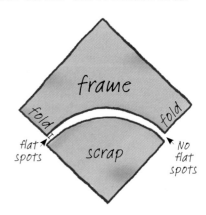

frame / scrap / flat spots / NO flat spots

Circle Sally says:
Be sure you place the Circle tool so one side is on the ¼″ seam side, but the other is on the fold line.

Half Circle Rectangle

22

Half Circle Rectangles

You'll make two half circle rectangles.

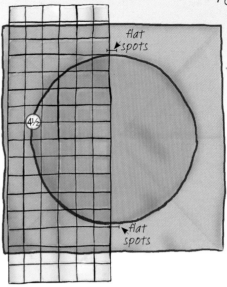

Fold and press both the circle and frame to mark eight equal divisions.

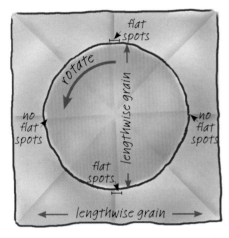

With the circle and frame on a flat surface, rotate the lengthwise grain of the circle perpendicular to the lengthwise grain of the frame.

With right sides together, match and pin the fold marks.

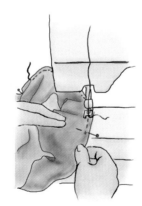

Sew the layers together with **exact** ¼" seams.

Press the seam allowance gently toward the frame, leaving the fold lines visible.

Place the ruler lines parallel to the edges of the fabric with the seam on the 4 ½" line.

Your fold lines will help you align your ruler. Be sure to keep your center point visible.

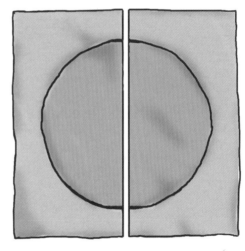

Trim each block to make an exact 6" x 11 ½" rectangle. Trim **only** from the frame sides.

You'll have even more block design possibilities if you'll reverse the frame and circle fabrics.

Half Circle Rectangle

Full Circle Block

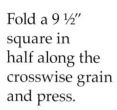

Fold a 9 ½"
square in
half along the
crosswise grain
and press.

9 ½" square — fold / fold

Fold the square in half again and press.

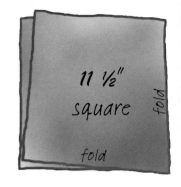

Fold a 11 ½"
square in
half along the
crosswise grain
and press.

11 ½" square — fold / fold

Fold the square in half again and press.

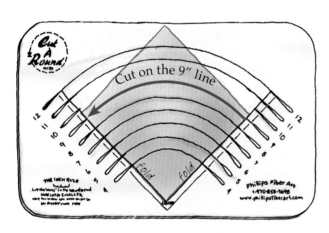

Cut on the 9" line

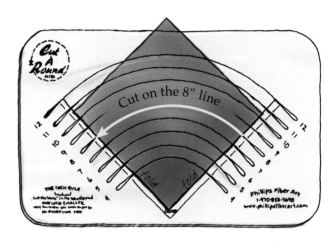

Cut on the 8" line

Place the *Cut A Round* tool on the fabric so
the folds are aligned with the **fold** lines.
Note: there are no flat spots on this circle.
Cut along the 9" curved slot.

Place the *Cut A Round* tool on the fabric so
the folds are aligned with the **fold** lines.
Note: there are no flat spots on this frame.
Cut along the 8" curved slot.

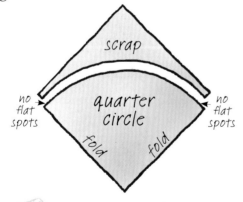

scrap

quarter circle

no flat spots — no flat spots

fold / fold

frame

scrap

no flat spots — no flat spots

fold / fold

Drunkard's Path

Full Circle

Circle Sally says:
A framed circle is a great
showcase for beautiful fabrics
and embroidery.

For more circle ideas
refer to the book,
Circle A Round.
See page 64.

Full Circle Block

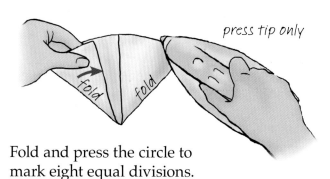

Fold and press the circle to mark eight equal divisions.

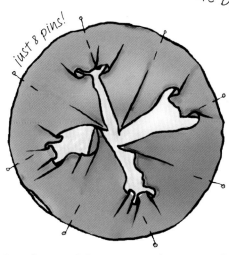

just 8 pins!

Bring frame fabric toward center of circle and with right sides together match and pin the fold marks.

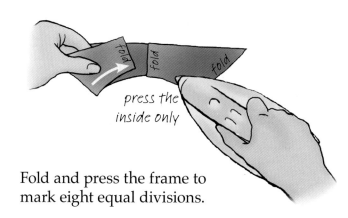

press the inside only

Fold and press the frame to mark eight equal divisions.

Adjust the edges of the frame to meet the circle. Bumps and uneven seam width will keep your circle from lying flat.

Sew the layers together with **exact** ¼" seams.

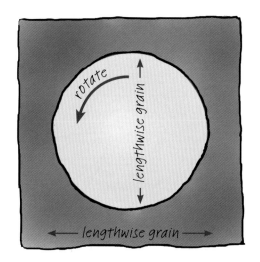

rotate

lengthwise grain

lengthwise grain

With the circle and frame on a flat surface, rotate the lengthwise grain of the circle perpendicular to the lengthwise grain of the frame.

A Full Circle Block

Full Circle

Pieced Double Path Drunkard's Path
Cutting a Circle

You'll cut a 9" circle from a 10" square of circle fabric.

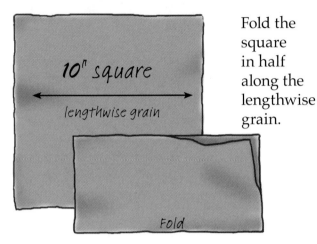

Fold the square in half along the lengthwise grain.

Press the fold.

To make grain lines easy to identify, always make your first fold along the lengthwise grain, to give it the strongest crease.

Fold it in half and press again.

This fold is along the crosswise grain.

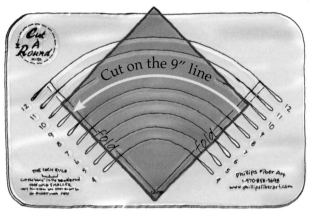

Place the *Cut A Round* tool on the fabric so the folds are aligned with the ¼" seam allowance lines.

Cut along the 9" curved slot.

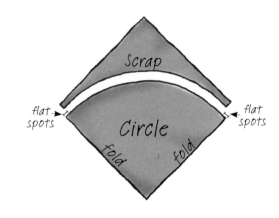

Scrap

flat spots | *flat spots*

Circle

fold | *fold*

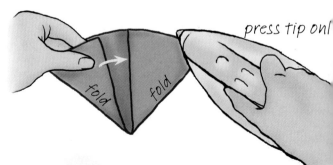

press tip onl

Fold and press the circle to mark eight equal divisions.

Circle Sally says:
The key to a perfect circle is to first fold and press the fabric into exact quarters.

Pieced Double Path Drunkard's Path
Cutting a Frame

You'll cut a 8" hole in a 12 ½" square of frame fabric.

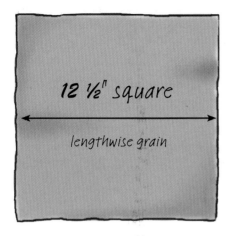

Cut a 12 ½" square of frame fabric.

12 ½" square

lengthwise grain

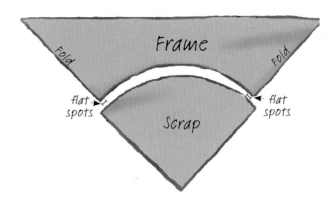

Frame

Fold   *Fold*

flat spots   flat spots

Scrap

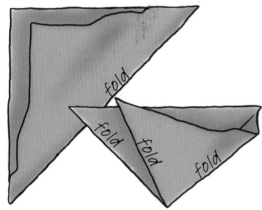

fold *fold* *fold* *fold*

Fold the frame fabric square in half diagonally.

Press the fold, being careful not to stretch it along the bias grain.

Fold it in half and press again.

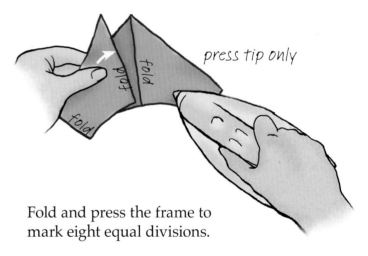

press tip only

fold *fold* *fold*

Fold and press the frame to mark eight equal divisions.

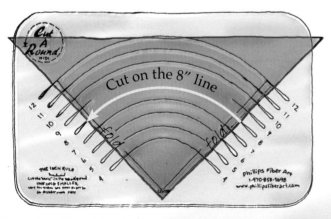

Cut A Round

Cut on the 8" line

fold *fold*

Phillips Fiber Art
1-970-858-1698
www.phillipsfiberart.com

Place the *Cut A Round* tool on the fabric so the folds are aligned with the ¼" seam allowance lines.

Cut along the 8" curved slot.

Pieced Double Path

Pieced Double Path Drunkard's Path
Framing a Circle

You'll sew the circle into the frame.

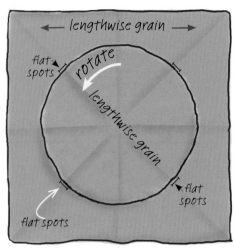

With the circle and frame on a flat surface, rotate the circle 45 degrees, so the "flat spots" of the circle match the "flat spots" of the frame.

*The frame differs from the previous Drunkard's Path Block.
The flat spots are on the diagonal rather than on the vertical and horizontal.*

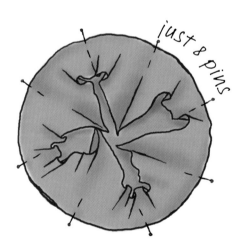

just 8 pins

Bring the frame fabric toward the center of the circle, right sides together, matching the fold marks.
Pin each matching fold mark.

Adjust the edges of the frame to meet the circle. Bumps and uneven seam width will keep your circle from lying flat.

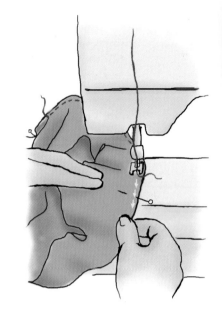

Sew the layers together with an exact ¼" seam. The circle is on the bottom against the bed of the machine and the frame is on top.

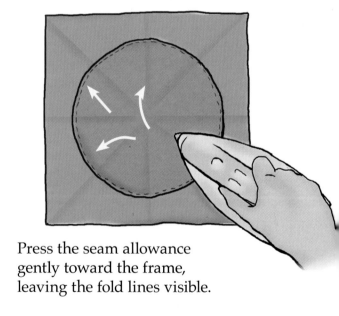

Press the seam allowance gently toward the frame, leaving the fold lines visible.

Circle Sally reminders:

√ ¼" seams must be exact.
√ Use your machine's needle-down feature.
√ The circle goes on bottom.

Pieced Double Path

28

© Cheryl Phillips and Karla Schulz

Pieced Double Path Drunkard's Path
Cutting Blocks

You'll cut the framed circle into four triangles.

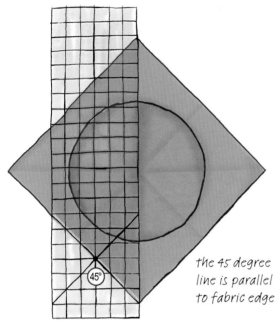

the 45 degree line is parallel to fabric edge

Your fold lines will help you align your ruler. Be sure to keep your center point visible.

You've completed four diagonal Drunkard's Path triangles at once!

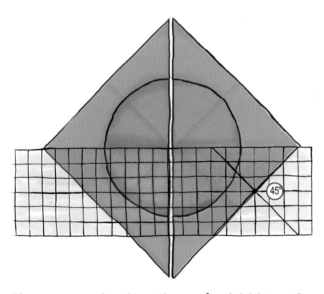

Place your ruler directly on the fold line of the framed circle square.

You can sew the triangles into two 8 ½" Double Path Block variations or any of the blocks and borders shown on pages 39 to 43.

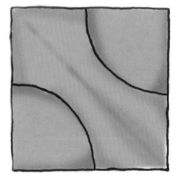

A Pieced Double Path Block

© Cheryl Phillips and Karla Schulz

Individual Double Path Block

You'll cut away two corners from a square and set in quarter circles.

Cut two 5" squares for the quarter circles.

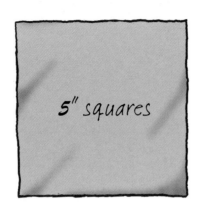

5" squares

8½" square

Cut an 8 ½" square for the frame.

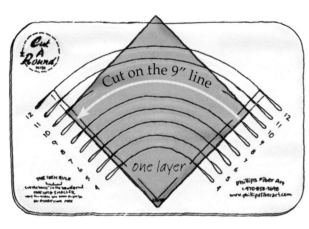

Cut on the 9" line

one layer

Place the *Cut A Round* tool on top of each fabric square. Align the fabric edge to the ¼" placement line.

Cut along the 9" slot for each quarter circle.

Cut two quarter circle pieces.

scrap

quarter circle

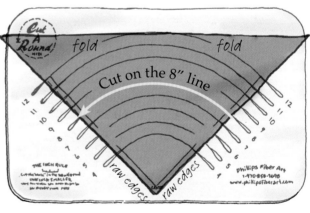

fold   fold

Cut on the 8" line

raw edges   raw edges

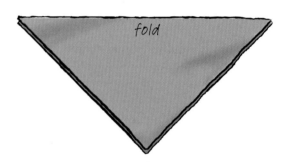

fold

Fold the square in half diagonally.

Place the *Cut A Round* tool on top of the folded fabric square. Place the folded side to the top and align the fabric edges to the ¼" placement line.

Cut along the 8" curved slot.

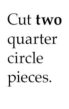

Individual Double Path Block

You'll sew two quarter circles into one square.

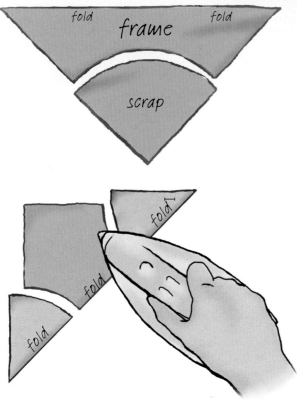

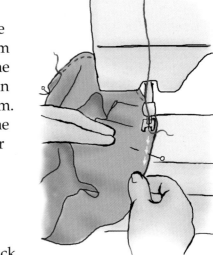

With the quarter circle on the bottom and the frame on top sew an exact ¼″ seam. Repeat for the other quarter circle.

Press the block.

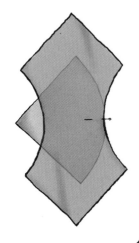

Fold the frame and the quarter circles in half. Press to mark the center of each piece.

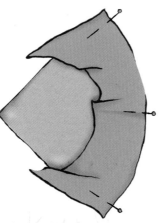

With right sides together match the center marks and pin. Match each side and pin.

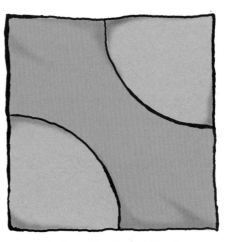

A Double Path Block

Individual Double Path

Uneven Double Path Block

You'll cut two different quarter circles and a frame.

Cut two squares for the quarter circles.

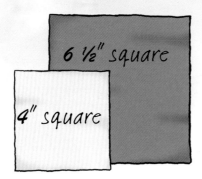

Cut an 8 ½" square for the frame.

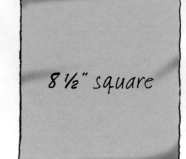

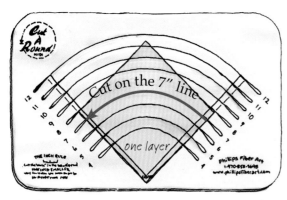

Place the *Cut A Round* tool on top of each fabric square. Align the fabric edge to the ¼" placement line.
Cut along the 7" slot for one quarter circle.

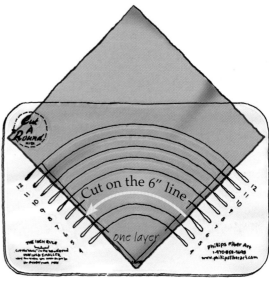

Place the *Cut A Round* tool on top of the fabric square. Align the fabric edge to the ¼" placement line.
Cut along the 6" line for the first corner.

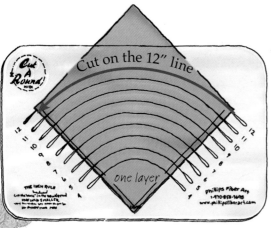

Cut along the 12" line for the other quarter circle.

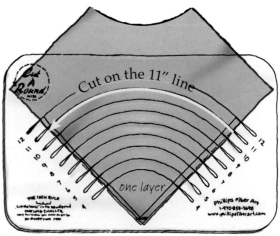

Cut along the 11" line for the other corner.

Uneven Double Path Block

You'll sew two quarter circles in one square.

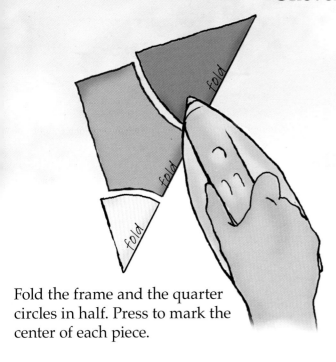

Fold the frame and the quarter circles in half. Press to mark the center of each piece.

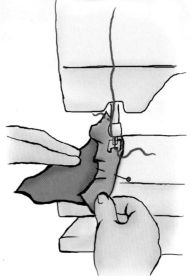

With the quarter circle on the bottom and the frame on top sew an exact ¼" seam. Repeat for the other quarter circle.

Press the block.

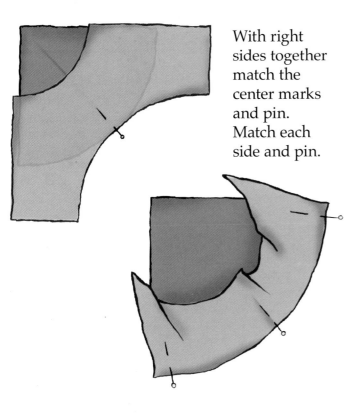

With right sides together match the center marks and pin. Match each side and pin.

Sew the smaller quarter circle to the frame in the same manner.

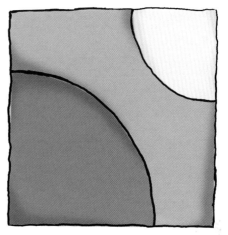

An Uneven Double Path Block

Uneven Double Path

Half Circle Triangles

Fold a 10″ square in half along the **crosswise** grain and press.

Fold the square in half again and press.

Fold a 12 ½″ square in half diagonally and press.

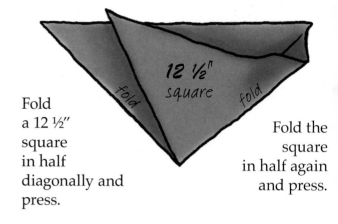

Fold the square in half again and press.

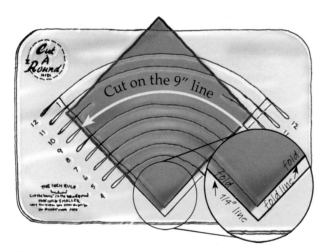

Place the *Cut A Round* tool on the fabric so one fold is aligned with the ¼″ seam allowance line and the other fold is aligned with the fold line on the tool.

Cut along the 9″ curved slot.

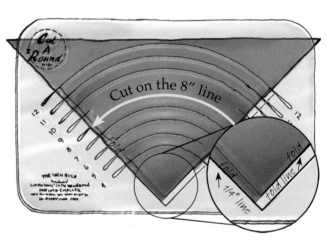

Place the *Cut A Round* tool on the fabric so one fold is aligned with the ¼″ seam allowance line and the other fold is aligned with the fold line on the tool.

Cut along the 8″ curved slot.

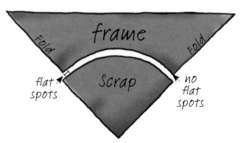

Circle Sally says:
Double check how you place the Circle tool—one side is on the ¼″ seam side, but the other is on the fold line.

34

Half Circle Triangles

You'll make two half circle triangles.

Fold and press both the circle and frame to mark the eighths.

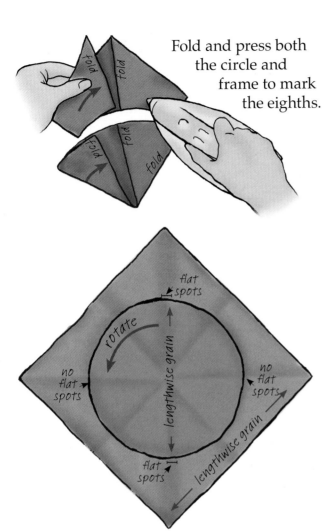

With the circle and frame on a flat surface, rotate the lengthwise grain of the circle. With right sides together, match and pin the fold marks.

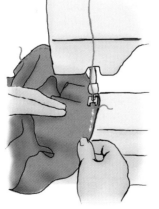

Sew the layers together with **exact** ¼″ seams.

Press the seam allowance gently toward the frame, leaving the fold lines visible.

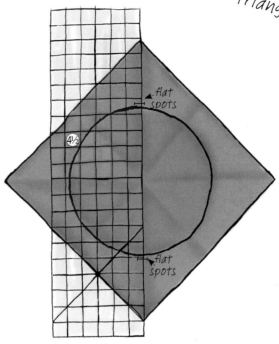

Place the ruler lines parallel to the edges of the fabric with the seam on the 4 ½″ line.

Your fold lines will help you align your ruler. Be sure to keep your center point visible.

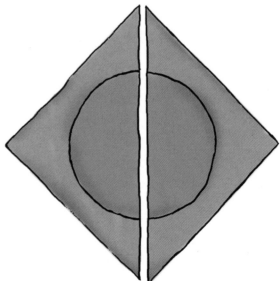

You'll have even more block design possibilities if you'll reverse the frame and circle fabrics.

Half Circle Triangles

Paths of Possibility

Let's play What if......?

What if you framed a circle?

What if you reversed the colors?

What if you mixed up the squares?

What if you added details?

Drunkard's Path

More What If......?

Asking What if is a great creative tool!

© Cheryl Phillips and Karla Schulz

37

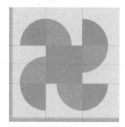
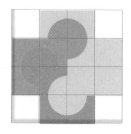
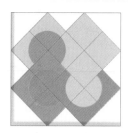

....you added plain squares? ....a pieced square? ...combined colors? ...put the blocks on point?

What if......

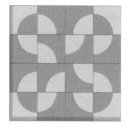
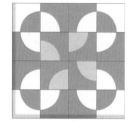
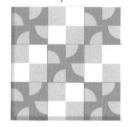

....you added blocks around the 4 patch? ....you added a third color? ....a pieced square?

Anita Murphy's Curved Nouveau

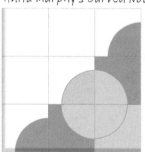
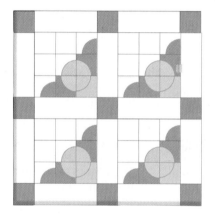
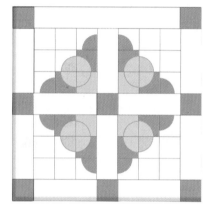

....you made a multi color block with plain squares? ....you added lattice and corner stones? ....you rotated the blocks?

Path in the Corner block

Full Circle block

The Path in the Corner and Full Circle are ideal for large scale fabrics.

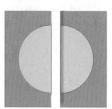

Half Circle Rectangle

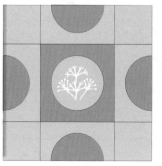

© Cheryl Phillips and Karla Schulz

Paths of Possibility

Play the "What if...?" game with diagonally cut squares.

What if you....

....reverse the colors?

......make 4 patch blocks?

.....rotate?

......reassemble?

....and on and on....?

Diagonal Set Blocks

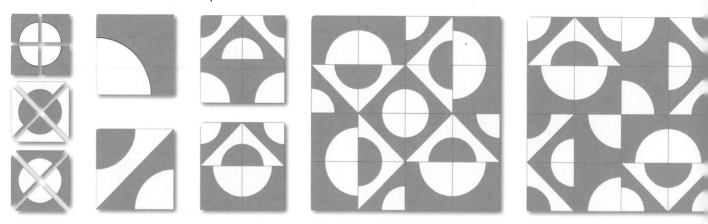

Combining straight set and diagonal set blocks offer endless possibilities.

While the four patch design may not be appealing by itself, look at the interesting results you get when you make four and rotate them?

Adding more colors gives the design flair.

Placing a square in the center, then rotating blocks around it offers a piecing challenge, but the results have such movement.

Drunkard's Path triangles sewn around a center square will require trimming to make the square.
Half circle rectangles frame the pinwheel block.

Straight set blocks rotated around a center square.

Lattice and cornerstones separate the pinwheels.

Contrasting rectangles create a design within the design.

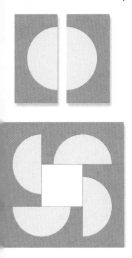

If Circle Rectangles

The Half Circle Rectangles are framed with Double Path blocks.

Double Path blocks replace the center squares.

When straight set blocks shown in the instructions are sewn together they make 6" squares. When the diagonal set blocks shown in the instructions are sewn together they make 8 ½" square. To mix and match the two types, you have to either make the straight set blocks larger or the diagonal set blocks smaller.

Straight Set Conversion Chart

To fit with the 8 ½" Diagonal set blocks, make the 6" Straight Set blocks larger.

Block	Page	Size	Size for Larger 8 ½" Block
Straight Set: Circle	12	9" circle from 10" sq	**13" circle from 14" sq**
Straight Set: Frame	13	12 ½" sq with 8" hole	**17" sq with 12" hole**
Ringed Inner Circle	16	7" circle from 8 ½" sq	**9" circle from 10" sq**
Ring Frame step	16	10" sq with 6" hole	**14" sq with 8" hole**
Ring Circle step	17	9" circle from a 10" sq	**13" circle from 14" sq**
Ringed Frame	17	12 ½" sq with 8" hole	**17" sq with 12" hole**
Single: Qtr Circle	18	9" arc from 5" sq	**13" arc from a 7" sq**
Single: Frame	18	6" sq with a 8" arc	**8 ½" sq with 12" arc**
Path in the Corner: Qtr Circle	20	9" arc from 5" sq	**13" arcs from 7" sqs**
Path in the Corner: Frame	20	11 ½" sq with 8" arcs	**16 ½" sq with 12" arcs**
Half Circle Rectangle: Circle	22	9" circle from 10" sq	**13" circle from 14" sq**
Half Circle Rectangle: Frame	22	12 ½" sq with 8" hole	**17" sq with 12" hole**
Full Circle: Circle	24	9" circle from 9 ½" sq	**13" circle from 14" sq**
Full Circle: Frame	24	11 ½" sq with 8" hole	**16 ½" sq with 12" hole**

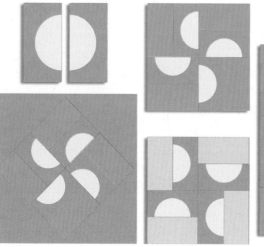

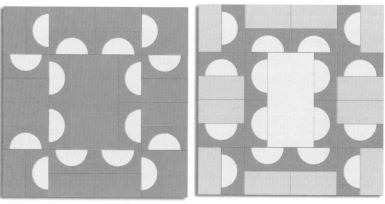

Half Circle Rectangles Drunkard's Path frames

Diagonal Set Conversion Chart

To fit with the 6" Straight set blocks make the 8 ½" Diagonal Set blocks smaller.

Block	Page	Size	Size for Smaller 6" Block
Pieced Double Path: Circle	26	9" circle from 10" sq	**7" circle from 8" sq**
Pieced Double Path: Frame	27	12 ½" sq with 8" hole	**9" sq with 6" hole**
Individual Double Path: Circle	30	9" arc from a 5" sq	**7" arc from 4" sq**
Individual Double Path: Frame	30	8 ½" sq with 8" arcs	**6" sq with 6" arcs**
Uneven Double: Small Qtr Circle	32	7" arc from 4" sq	**6" arc from 4" sq**
Uneven Double: Small Frame	32	8 ½" sq with 6" arc	**6" sq with 5" arc**
Uneven Double: Large Qtr Circle	32	12" arc from 6 1/2" sq	**9" arc from 5" sq**
Uneven Double: Large Frame	32	8 ½" sq with 6" arc	**6" sq with 8" arc**
Half Circle Triangle: Qtr Circle	34	9" circle from 10" sq	**7" circle from 8" sq**
Half Circle Triangle: Frame	34	12 ½" sq with 8" hole	**9" sq with 6" hole**

Half Diagonal and Triangle Drunkard's Path blocks make great borders and frames

Diagonal Delights   *(Above and Right)*
Pieced Double Path blocks were so much fun, we just couldn't stop making blocks!

© Cheryl Phillips and Karla Schulz

Drunkard's Path

Birds in Flight Formation
made with Straight and Diagonal Set Blocks.

Triangle Weave
Half Circle Triangle Blocks simply sewn in rows.

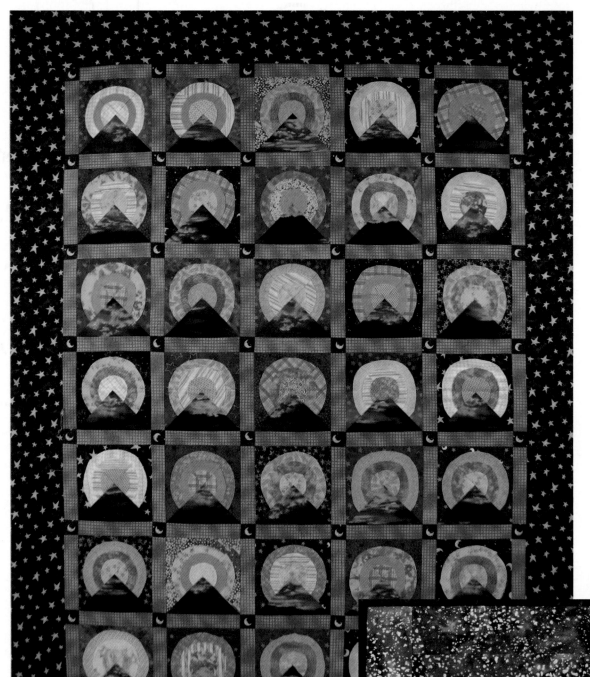

Many Moons over Greenhorn Mountain
(left)

Drunkard's Path Triangles made with true circles without flat spots sewn with raw edge applique to add folk charm.

Moon over the Mountain
(right)

made with Drunkard's Path Triangle Blocks and a plain triangle.

48

Drunkard's Path

Asian Gold
(left)
Path in the Corner Blocks feature
solid fabric centers surrounded by
two gold tones.

Tuscan Bell Pull
(below)

Individual Double Path blocks
on point.

Amber Roses
(left)

Ringed Paths are used in the
Path in the Corner block and are
bordered by Diagonal Set and Half
Circle Triangle blocks.

49

Celtic Rings with Circling Geese

Drunkard's Path blocks provide a background for Kathy Moorehead Johnson's piecing and Celtic applique.

Circling South

Drunkard's Path blocks provide a background for soaring flying geese in various shades of hand dyed fabrics.

Be inspired by Kathy's talents at www.augustwindquiltdesigns.com

50

Drunkard's Path

Within the handkerchief image:
Keegan Michael
May 7, 2001

Hunter Phillip
February 19, 2001

Savanna Riley
May 5, 2005

Chayse Marie
May 11, 2006

Brigan Paul
January 19, 2005

Twirl and Swirl
Diagonal Set triangles spin around center squares

Grammy's Handkerchief
Path in the Corner blocks showcase fussy cut Northcott handkerchief fabrics.

Scraps, Scraps, and More Scraps

How many blocks...?
How many quilts...?
can you make
if you go
through
your pile
of scraps
cutting
circles as
you go?

Diagonal Puzzle
Made with larger 8 ½" Ringed Drunkard's Path blocks

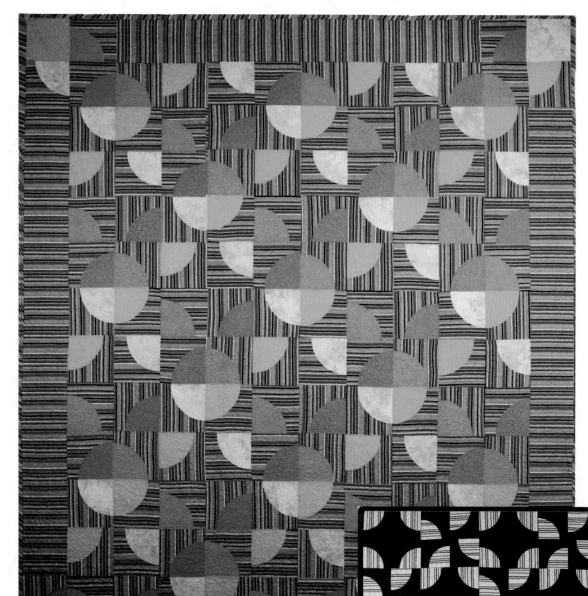

What to do you do with all those scrap circles?

Two for one Quilts

Circles of several colors with striped frames are used for the first quilt. Leftover striped background circles were raw edge appliquéd to black dot background squares, then cut into Drunkard's Path Blocks for a second quilt.

Drunkard's Path

Dot Candy
(below)
uses the Uneven
Double Path block.

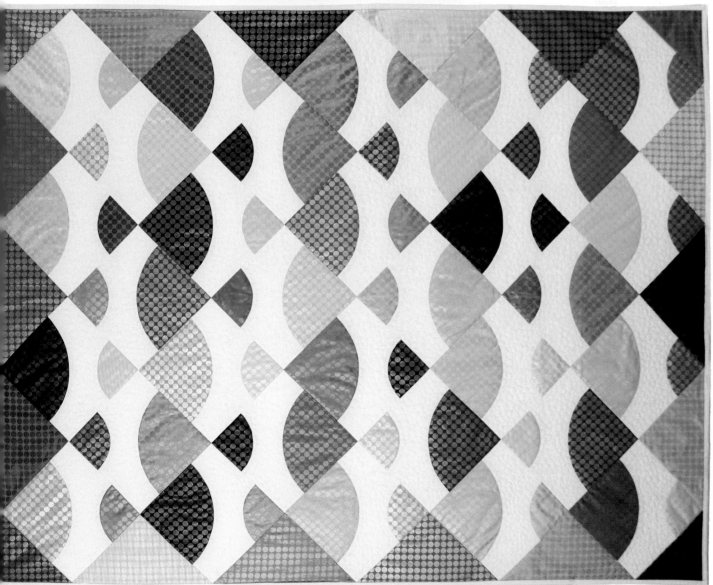

Table Runners
use Straight Set
Drunkard Path blocks
made with the same
sized frame, but
different circle sizes.

Woolly Remembrance
Remnants from many wool projects sewn together into a hand tied memory collection.

Rob Petra
to Pay Pao
(left)

a mix and match
arrangement
of Asian
Lakehouse
fabrics.

Chess Pieces

(right)

Sewn with Half Circle Rectangle
blocks in Northcott Aviary fabric.

Round About
Straight Set Drunkard's Path blocks in a carefree block arrangement

Trail Mix
Large Ringed blocks together with Diagonal Set blocks and solid squares create a visual dance.

Templates

You can substitute the following templates for the *Cut A Round* tool. Refer to the appropriate block pattern page for each template, carefully following cutting instructions.

Trace the templates onto freezer paper. Iron the paper onto your fabric, then cut out both paper and fabric in one step. Scissors will work better than a rotary cutter here. Keep in mind how important it is to be accurate with your cutting.

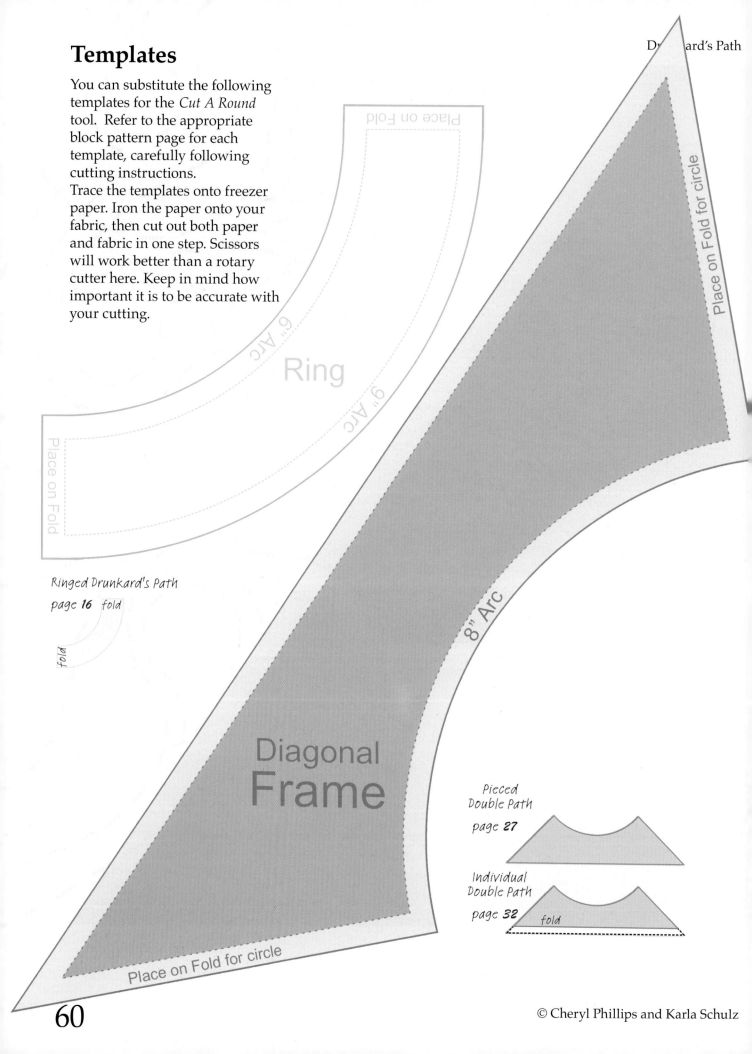

Place on Fold

Place on Fold

6" Arc

9" Arc

Ring

Place on Fold

Ringed Drunkard's Path

page **16**   fold

fold

fold

Drunkard's Path

Place on Fold for circle

8" Arc

Diagonal
Frame

Pieced
Double Path

page **27**

Individual
Double Path

page **32**   fold

Place on Fold for circle

60

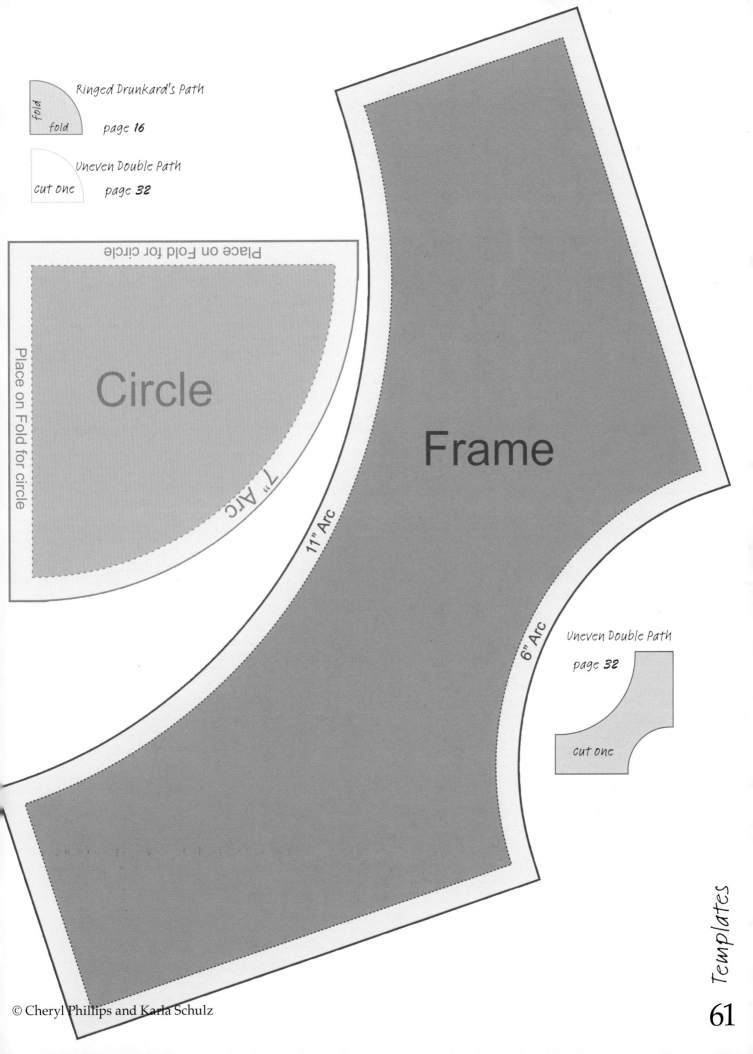

Ringed Drunkard's Path

page **16**

fold

fold

Uneven Double Path

cut one

page **32**

Place on Fold for circle

Place on Fold for circle

Circle

Place on Fold for circle

7" Arc

11" Arc

Frame

6" Arc

Uneven Double Path

page **32**

cut one

Templates

61

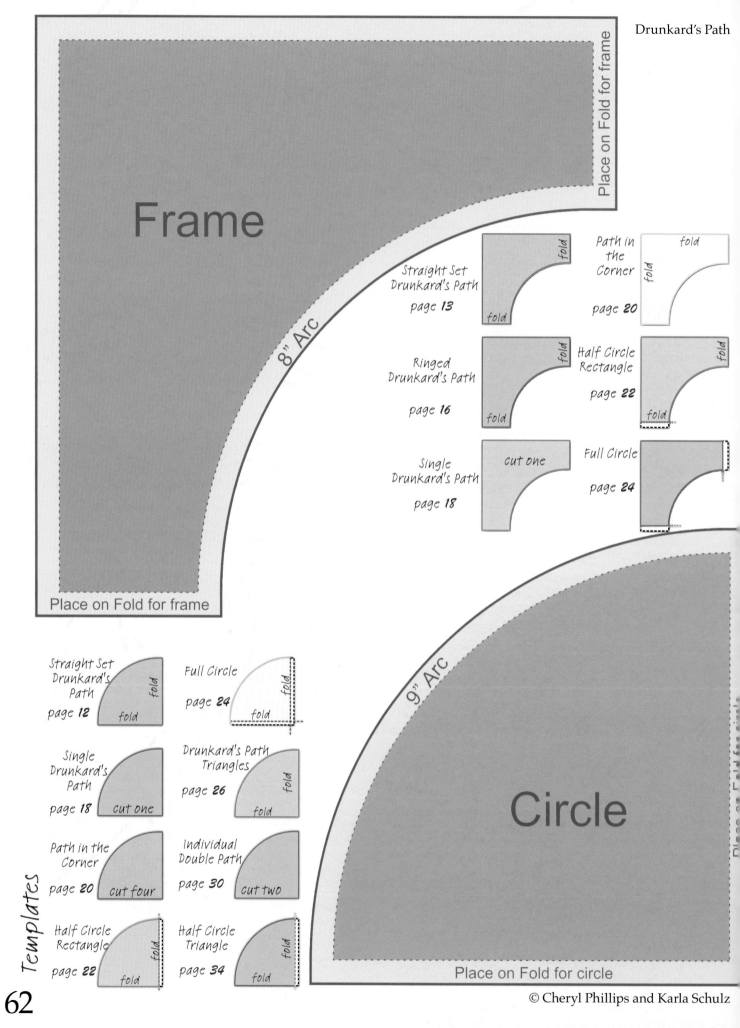

Drunkard's Path

Frame

Place on Fold for frame

Place on Fold for frame

8" Arc

9" Arc

Circle

Place on Fold for circle

Straight Set Drunkard's Path
page *13*
fold

Path in the Corner
page *20*
fold

Ringed Drunkard's Path
page *16*
fold

Half Circle Rectangle
page *22*
fold

Single Drunkard's Path
page *18*
cut one

Full Circle
page *24*

Templates

Straight Set Drunkard's Path
page *12*
fold

Full Circle
page *24*
fold

Single Drunkard's Path
page *18*
cut one

Drunkard's Path Triangles
page *26*
fold

Path in the Corner
page *20*
cut four

Individual Double Path
page *30*
cut two

Half Circle Rectangle
page *22*
fold

Half Circle Triangle
page *34*
fold

62

© Cheryl Phillips and Karla Schulz

Drunkard's Path

Uneven Double Path

page **32**

cut one

Circle

12" Arc

If you want to change block sizes, here is a chart giving you the correct proportions for other sizes:

A	B	Individual Block
4" circle from a 5" square	5 1/2" square with a 3" hole	2 3/4" square
5" circle from a 6" square	7" square with a 4" hole	3 1/2" square
6" circle from a 7" square	8 1/2" square with a 5" hole	4 1/4" square
7" circle from a 8" square	9 1/2" square with a 6" hole	4 3/4" square
8" circle from a 9" square	11" square with a 7" hole	5 1/2" square
9" circle from a 10" square	12 1/2" square with a 8" hole	6 1/4" square
10" circle from a 11" square	14" square with a 9" hole	7" square
11" circle from a 12" square	15" square with a 10" hole	5 1/2" square
12" circle from a 11" square	16 1/2" square with a 11" hole	8 1/4" square
13" circle from a 12" square	18" square with a 12" hole	9" square

Templates

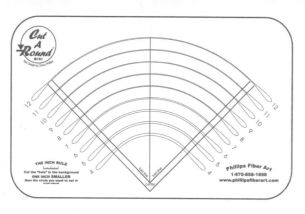

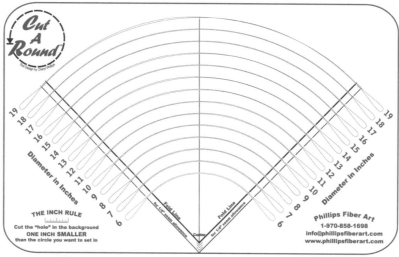

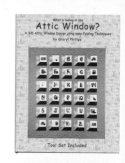

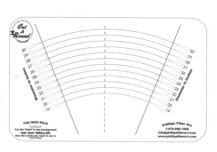

Cut A Round tools
Standard size for circles 6" to 19"
Portable Midi size for circles 4" to 12"
Large size for circles 19" to 30"
Mini size for circles 2" to 8"

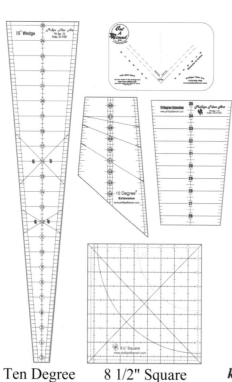

Ten Degree
Wedge

8 1/2" Square

Phillips Fiber Art
PO Box 173
Fruita, CO 81521
www.phillipsfiberart.com
info@phillipsfiberart.com

Karla Schulz
87309 580th Ave.
Jackson, MN 56143
kdschulz@federatedwildblue.com

64